# THE CATCHER IN THE RYE

by
J.D. Salinger

## Student Packet

Written by
Gloria Levine, M.A.

**Contains masters for:**

| | |
|---|---|
| 1 | Anticipation Guide |
| 1 | Study Guide  (5 pages) |
| 7 | Vocabulary Activities |
| 2 | Critical Thinking Activities |
| 4 | Creative Writing Activities |
| 5 | Literary Analysis Activities |
| 2 | Comprehension Quizzes  (two levels) |
| 2 | Unit Exams  (two levels) |

**PLUS**  Detailed Answer Key

---

### Note

The text used to prepare this guide was the softcover published by Little, Brown, & Co., ©1945, 1946, and 1951 by J.D. Salinger. The page references may differ in other editions.

**Please note:** Please assess the appropriateness of this book for the age level and maturity of your students prior to reading and discussing it with your class.

---

**Copyright infringement is a violation of Federal Law.**

© 2000 by Novel Units, Inc., Bulverde, Texas. All rights reserved. No part of this publication may be reproduced, translated, stored in a retrieval system, or transmitted in any way or by any means (electronic, mechanical, photocopying, recording, or otherwise) without prior written permission from Novel Units, Inc.

Photocopying of student worksheets by a classroom teacher at a non-profit school who has purchased this publication for his/her own class is permissible. Reproduction of any part of this publication for an entire school or for a school system, by for-profit institutions and tutoring centers, or for commercial sale is strictly prohibited.

Novel Units is a registered trademark of Novel Units, Inc.  Printed in the United States of America.

To order, contact your local school supply store, or—

Novel Units, Inc.
P.O. Box 97
Bulverde, TX 78163-0097

Web site: www.educyberstor.com

# Anticipation Guide

**Directions:** Rate each of the following statements before you read the novel. Compare your ratings with a partner's, and discuss why you chose the particular ratings you did. (After you have completed the novel, discuss with your partner whether you would change any of the ratings.)

1 ———— 2 ———— 3 ———— 4 ———— 5 ———— 6

agree strongly                                    strongly disagree

1. _____ People always think something's all true.

2. _____ People tend to notice when you act younger than you are, not when you act older than you are.

3. _____ Handsome guys are always asking you to do them a favor.

4. _____ If you're good at writing compositions, there's always somebody who will start talking about how you know all the rules of grammar and punctuation.

5. _____ Jocks always hang out together.

6. _____ Almost every time somebody gives me a present it ends up making me sad.

7. _____ It's okay to tell a lie if it makes somebody feel good.

8. _____ The girls/guys I like best in a romantic way are the ones I never feel much like kidding.

9. _____ If you want to stay alive, you have to say stuff like "Glad to have met you" when you don't really mean it.

10. _____ I never care too much when I lose something.

11. _____ Money always ends up making you blue.

12. _____ If a girl likes a boy, she'll excuse his obnoxiousness by saying he has an inferiority complex.

13. _____ If a girl doesn't like a boy, no matter how nice he is or how big an inferiority complex he has, she'll say he's conceited.

14. _____ Mothers are all slightly insane.

15. _____ The mark of an immature man is that he wants to die nobly for a cause, while the mark of the mature man is that he wants to live humbly for one.

# Study Questions

Write a brief answer to each study question as you read the novel at home or in class. Use the questions for review before group discussions and before your final exam.

**Chapter 1**
1. Who is the narrator? About what does he promise to tell the reader?
2. Who is D. B.? Why does the narrator call him a "prostitute"?
3. What is Pencey Prep?
4. Why is the narrator leaving Pencey? How does he feel about leaving?

**Chapter 2**
1. Who is Mr. Spencer? Why does Holden visit him?
2. How does Holden describe himself, physically?
3. Why does Mr. Spencer read the essay about Egyptians? How does Holden react to hearing the paper read?
4. What are Whooton and Elkton Hills? Why did Holden leave them?

**Chapter 3**
1. What did Holden buy in New York after losing the foils?
2. Name three authors whose work Holden has read. Do you enjoy these writers?
3. Who is Ackley? Does the narrator seem to like him? Would you?
4. Who is Stradlater? Briefly describe him.

**Chapter 4**
1. What favor does Stradlater ask of the narrator?
2. Who is Stradlater's date?
3. How does Holden happen to know Jane? How does he seem to feel about Stradlater's dating her?

**Chapter 5**
1. Where does Holden go on Saturday night? What does he end up doing?
2. What topic does Holden choose for the composition he is writing for Stradlater?
3. Who was Allie? What sort of person was he? How did Holden feel about him?
4. In what year did Allie die? How much time has passed? How old is Holden now? How old would Allie have been?

**Chapter 6**
1. Why is Holden worrying when Stradlater returns?
2. Why doesn't Stradlater like the composition? What happens?

**Chapter 7**
1. Why does Holden go to Ackley's room?
2. Why does Holden call Ackley a "prince...gentleman...and a scholar"?

3. Why does Holden decide to leave Pencey in the middle of the night—days earlier than he had planned? Where does he plan to go?

## Chapter 8
1. Who sits next to Holden on the train?
2. What lies does Holden tell the mother about her son? Why?
3. How does Holden explain the fact that he is not in school?

## Chapter 9
1. List the people Holden thinks of calling from Penn Station.
2. What does Holden ask the taxi driver about the ducks?
3. What sorts of "perverts" does Holden see at the hotel?
4. What "sex rule" has Holden made for himself? Why does he break it?
5. Who is "Miss Faith Cavendish"? Why doesn't Holden arrange to meet her?

## Chapter 10
1. What does Holden like about his sister Phoebe?
2. What does Holden order to drink at the Lavender Room? Why does he end up drinking Coke instead?
3. What does Holden think of the three women he meets in the Lavender Room?

## Chapter 11
1. Why do you think Holden can't stop thinking about Jane Gallagher?
2. How is Jane different from most of the girls Holden knows?

## Chapter 12
1. Who is Horwitz? What do he and Holden talk about?
2. Who is Ernie? Why does Holden consider him "phony"? Why, then, do you think he sends Ernie a message inviting him over for a drink?
3. Who is Lillian Simmons? What does Holden think of her?
4. On page 86, Holden says: "People are always ruining things for you." Why? Who has ruined what for him?

## Chapter 13
1. What would Holden have done if he found out who stole his gloves? Why does he consider himself "yellow"? Do you think he is a coward?
2. How is Holden feeling when he gets back to the hotel?
3. What is the "big mess" Holden gets into when he steps onto the elevator?

## Chapter 14
1. Why does Holden "talk to Allie" after Sunny leaves? Why does Holden "tell" Allie "go home and get your bike and meet me in front of Bobby Fallon's house"?
2. What are Holden's religious beliefs?

3. Who is Maurice and why does he knock on Holden's door? Do you think Holden does the best thing under the circumstances?
4. After Maurice leaves, how does Holden feel? Why doesn't he jump out a window as he considers doing?

## Chapter 15
1. Who is Sally Hayes? Does Holden like her? What does he think of her?
2. What is your impression of Holden's father?
3. Why does Holden start thinking about Dick Slagle?
4. What is Holden's opinion of the nuns in the train station? Are you surprised that he doesn't find them "phony"?

## Chapter 16
1. Why does Holden walk down Broadway looking for a record store?
2. What is the little boy who is walking with his parents singing? Does that make Holden feel better or worse?
3. How does Holden feel about movies and shows? Why doesn't he like actors?
4. Why did Holden like the museum so much as a kid? How does Holden seem to feel about change?

## Chapter 17
1. Who was Harris Macklin and why didn't Holden like him? Who else does he seem to label as a "bore"?
2. Why do you think Holden tells Sally he loves her in the cab on the way to the show? What is her response?
3. Why does Holden consider the Andover acquaintance Sally meets in the lobby a "phony"? Would you?
4. Why do Sally and Holden go skating? Do they have a good time?

## Chapter 18
1. What does Holden think of the Christmas show at Radio City Music Hall? Do you think you would enjoy that show?
2. Does Holden like the movie? Can you identify which movie it is?
3. How does Holden feel about going to war? Why do you suppose this is on his mind?

## Chapter 19
1. How does Holden know Carl Luce? What sorts of talks has he had with Carl in the past?
2. What does Holden dislike about Carl? Why does he make the effort to see him, then?
3. What does Carl think Holden needs? Do you think Carl is right?

## Chapter 20
1. What does Holden pretend while sitting at the bar?
2. Why is Holden "blind" when he calls Sally? What is her reaction when she answers the phone?
3. What is the "terrible thing" that happens when Holden leaves the bar?
4. Why did Holden miss Allie's funeral?

## Chapter 21
1. What does Holden do when he gets into the apartment and finds Phoebe asleep?
2. How can you tell that Phoebe is thrilled to see Holden? What bits of news does she shower on him?
3. Why does Phoebe put the pillow over her head?

## Chapter 22
1. When Phoebe asks Holden why he flunked out again, what does he respond? Do you think he is being honest? Do you think Holden would be happier at your school?
2. Who was James Castle? Why do you think Holden thinks of him when Phoebe asks him to name one thing he likes?
3. What two things does Holden say he likes? Why isn't Phoebe satisfied with his answer?
4. When Phoebe asks Holden what he'd like to be, what is his explanation for why he would NOT like to be a lawyer? What does this show about his relationship with his father?
5. What would Holden like to be? Why?

## Chapter 23
1. Who is Mr. Antolini? Why does Holden like him?
2. How do you learn that both Holden and Phoebe are good dancers?
3. What does Phoebe give Holden? Why do you think he cries?
4. Where does Holden decide to go? Why is he hiding from his parents until Wednesday?

## Chapter 24
1. What sort of talk does Mr. Antolini have with Holden about his flunking out? How is that talk similar to/different from the lecture Mr. Spencer gave him?
2. Who is Wilhelm Stekel and why does Mr. Antolini quote him? Do you think Holden would be better off if he took Mr. Antolini's advice to heart?
3. Why is Holden upset when he wakes up? Should he be? What do you think about "that kind of stuff's happened to me about twenty times since I was a kid"?

## Chapter 25

1. Where does Holden go after he leaves Mr. Antolini's?
2. Why does Holden feel worse after reading the article in the magazine about hormones? Do you worry more about your health when you are depressed?
3. Why does Holden laugh as he watches the men unloading the Christmas tree? How does he feel?
4. Why doesn't Holden eat the doughnuts he has ordered? Have you ever experienced anything like that when you were blue?
5. What is the "spooky thing" that happens to Holden as he is walking down Fifth Avenue?
6. What plan does Holden concoct for escaping from everything?
7. Why does Holden go to Phoebe's school? Why does the graffiti make him so angry?
8. How does Holden get along with the two little boys in the museum? Toward what other children in the story has he shown a similar attitude?
9. Why does Holden yell at Phoebe?
10. Why does Holden change his mind about going away?
11. Where do Holden and Phoebe go after their argument?
12. How does Holden feel as he watches Phoebe on the carrousel? Why?

## Chapter 26

1. What happens after Holden goes home? Why do you suppose Holden doesn't tell about that in more detail?
2. When is Holden going back to school? Do you think he will "apply himself"?
3. Where does Holden seem to be as he tells the story?
4. Who does D. B. bring along on his visit with Holden? What does D. B. talk with Holden about on that visit?
5. Holden says of "all that has happened": "I'm sorry I told so many people about it." Who has he told? Why do you suppose he is sorry?

| | | | |
|---|---|---|---|
| hemorrhages (1) | foils (3) | ostracized (3) | grippe (3) |
| chiffonier (11) | lagoon (13) | compulsory (17) | falsetto (23) |
| hound's tooth (25) | | | |

**Directions:** Group members decide who will be responsible for mapping which word(s) from the box above. Then turn to the page on which your word is used in the novel. After examining how the word is used in context, complete the word map and explain your finished map to other members of your group.

**Synonyms:**

_____
_____
_____
_____
_____

**Drawing or Other Visual that Represents the Meaning of the Word:**

**Word:**
_____

**Dictionary Definition:**
_____
_____
_____

**Word Used in a Sentence:**
_____
_____
_____
_____

Name_____

The Catcher in the Rye
Activity #3: Vocabulary
Chapters 4-7, pages 26-52

| ironical (28) | exhibitionist (29) | half nelson (30) | liberate (30) |
| caddy (32) | psychoanalyzed (39) | halitosis (39) | unscrupulous (40) |
| pacifist (46) | lavish (52) | | |

**Directions:** Below are four graphic organizers that show the relationships between several words. Choose the word from the box that best completes each organizer. Discuss your choices with other members of your group.

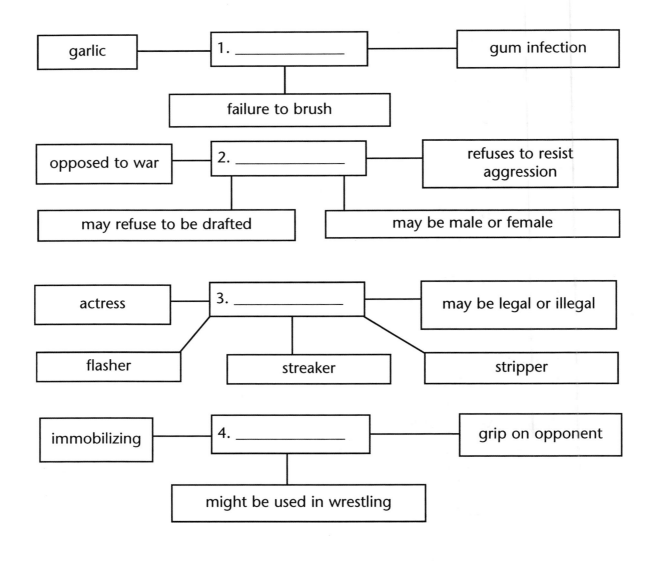

© Novel Units, Inc.

10

All rights reserved

| | | | |
|---|---|---|---|
| conscientious (55) | incognito (60) | suave (64) | verification (69) |
| conversationalist (72) | jitterbugging (72) | immaterial (72) | |

**Directions:** Circle the word from each list that does not belong with the others. Briefly explain why that word does not belong.

1. required     immaterial     compulsory     mandatory

_____

2. integrating     secluding     jitterbugging     ostracizing

_____

3. aimless     conscientious     suave     chivalrous

_____

4. conversationalist     chiffonier     armoire     dresser

_____

5. incognito     anonymous     disguised     muscular

_____

6. verification     affirmation     ostentation     documentation

_____

Name_____

chateau (93)          rake (93)          clavichord (96)

**Directions:** Use a plus (+) or minus (-) to identify the attributes of a chateau, a rake, a clavichord and other related words.

|  | scoundrel | cruel | impulsive |
|---|---|---|---|
| rake |  |  |  |
| tyrant |  |  |  |
| gent |  |  |  |
| lady |  |  |  |

|  | castle in France | mansion | stately |
|---|---|---|---|
| palace |  |  |  |
| villa |  |  |  |
| pueblo |  |  |  |
| chateau |  |  |  |

|  | early instrument | keyboard | soft sounds only | smallish |
|---|---|---|---|---|
| piano |  |  |  |  |
| organ |  |  |  |  |
| clavichord |  |  |  |  |
| moog synthesizer |  |  |  |  |

| | | |
|---|---|---|
| spendthrift (107) | bourgeois (108) | prejudiced (112) |
| mutinying (120) | raspy (123) | clique (131) |

**Directions:** Match each word or phrase below with a word in the *antonym* box above that means the *opposite.* Some words will be used twice.

1. _____ group open to all

2. _____ miser

3. _____ spiritual, refined

4. _____ mellow, musical

5. _____ unbiased

6. _____ remaining loyal

7. _____ would rather save than spend

8. _____ smooth

9. _____ accepting

10. _____ constant, faithful

Name_____

| | | | |
|---|---|---|---|
| inferiority complex | sacrilegious | atheist | kettle drums |
| putrid | celebrity | aristocratic | inane |
| spiritual | psychoanalyst | boisterous | economizing |

**Directions:** Match each word or phrase in the box above with one of the definitions below.

1. _____ rough and noisy

2. _____ hemispheres of metal covered with skin, tuned by foot pedals

3. _____ extreme reticence of aggressiveness resulting from feeling of low self-esteem

4. _____ person trained to investigate unconscious psychological processes

5. _____ in a state of foul decay

6. _____ violation of anything sacred

7. _____ frivolous, meaningless

8. _____ one who disbelieves the existence of God

9. _____ luminary, star

10. _____ blue-blooded, regal

11. _____ sanctified, celestial

12. _____ conserving, skimping

| intellectual | pedagogical | provocative | unify |
| harrowing | stenographer | reciprocal | humility |
| unsanitary | double-decker buses | | |

**Directions:** Fill in the blanks with words from the vocabulary box.

1. If you like feeling the wind in your hair, you will enjoy the _____ in England.

2. Being stuck in the elevator for two hours was a _____ experience.

3. We have a _____ arrangement; one week I watch her kids and the next week she watches mine.

4. It is a sign of his _____ that he never told anyone of his receiving the award.

5. At 92, she has not given up _____ pursuits; she reads avidly and is even taking a course in Russian history.

6. It is a highly _____ book that will really make you think about how the universe was created.

7. After you see the _____ conditions in the kitchen, you won't want to eat in that restaurant any more.

8. The decision to _____ East and West Germany has solved some problems and created others.

9. The minister was known for teaching the congregation by asking _____ questions from the pulpit.

10. The court _____ uses a special machine to take shorthand notes about the trial.

Name_____

**Directions:** Create an attribute web for Holden Caulfield. As you read, feel free to add more categories of your own, additional notes, etc.

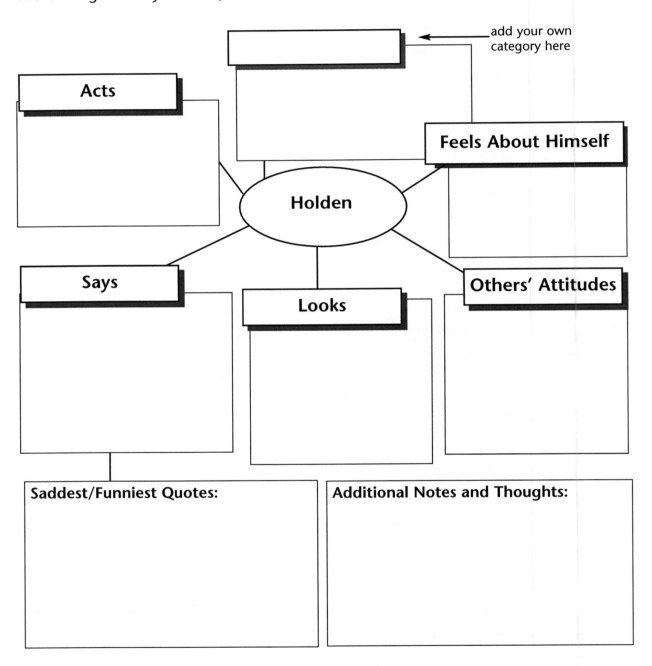

add your own category here

**Acts**

**Feels About Himself**

Holden

**Says**

**Looks**

**Others' Attitudes**

**Saddest/Funniest Quotes:**

**Additional Notes and Thoughts:**

# Setting

**Directions:** The events of the story take place in several different settings (times and places). Settings often reflect the mood—or even help set it.

A.  Complete the chart below by listing some of the settings in the story and the mood in each setting. The chart has been started for you.

| **Setting** | **Mood** |
|---|---|
| 1.  the Spencer house | gloomy, air of sickness |
| 2.  Pencey Prep (Holden's room) | |
| 3.  train to New York | |
| 4.  Grand Central Station | |
| 5.  _____ | |
| 6.  _____ | |
| 7.  _____ | |
| 8.  _____ | |
| 9.  _____ | |
| 10.  _____ | |

B.  For each of the settings above write one sentence about an event that takes place in that setting. (Use the back of your paper, and number your sentences to correspond with the numbers of the settings.)

**Directions:** In the final two chapters, we **do not** see what happens when Phoebe gets off the carrousel and goes home with Holden. In this exercise, you will write that scene, using details from the story and ideas from your own imagination.

**Pre-Writing:** A teacher or group leader should read the following directions. Students should relax, listen, and allow themselves to feel part of the scene. Before beginning to read, make sure students have paper and pens close at hand so they can make notes while their thoughts and feelings are fresh.

Take a few minutes to relax and imagine yourself as Holden, with Phoebe at the carrousel. Recreate that scene in your minds. Which animals do you imagine? What music is playing? What other sounds do you hear? Can you see the little kids going up and down—their parents sitting on the benches around the outside? What aromas do you notice? Walk through the scene. Go up to the ticket window. Watch Phoebe's face as you give her the tickets and try to give her her money back. Notice her pleading tones as she begs you to keep the money...and see her walk around the carrousel looking for just the right animal...and Phoebe is choosing the beat-up-horse...and the calliope is playing "Smoke Gets in Your Eyes"...and kids are grabbing for the gold ring...and you are aware of your fear that Phoebe will fall off...and the ride is over and Phoebe is asking you to get on, too...and she is telling you that she isn't mad anymore...and she is giving you a kiss...and putting your cap on your head and getting back on the carrousel just in time. You are aware of how happy you feel as you watch Phoebe...and how wet you are getting as the rain starts to pour down...and how much you feel like crying. And you can let the happenings flow in your mind for a few minutes until you realize how the next part of the story is taking shape. Do you and Phoebe go home right away? Who is home when you get there? What do you have to say to each other? Now return to the here and now, pick up your pen, and use the next few minutes to jot down some notes.

**Mid-Writing:** Write the scene that describes what happens next. Include some direct quotations and some narrative.

**Post-Writing:** Perform the scene with a few classmates. Discuss how the characters' dialogue could be altered to sound more natural—and more in keeping with their personalities.

## Writing Response:
## Narration of Personal Experience from Two Points of View

It is the night after Holden watched Phoebe ride on the carrousel. Write a journal entry about that day from Phoebe's point of view, and from Holden's.

**Pre-Writing: With a partner...**
1.  Discuss what the day has been like for Holden. Jot down ideas about the following: Where did Holden sleep this morning? What did he see on his walk? How was he feeling? What sort of fantasies did he have? Why did he arrange to have Phoebe meet him? How did Holden's plans change after he met Phoebe? Why did they argue? Where and how did they make up? What would Holden consider the high and low points of the day?

2.  Assume Phoebe's persona and reflect aloud on the events of the day. What sort of day might she have been having at school? How did she probably feel when she received Holden's note? How long did it take her to decide to pack her suitcase? How would Phoebe's view of the time at the carrousel be different from Holden's? What would Phoebe consider the high and low points of the day?

**Mid-Writing: On your own...**
1.  Write Holden's journal entry for the day. Remember that this is a private journal entry, so it will probably include both facts and feelings.

2.  Repeat, this time assuming Phoebe's persona.

**Post-Writing: With your class...**
Read your journal entries aloud to others. Discuss with them whether you have succeeded in assuming the points of view of Holden and Phoebe. Does the contrast in temperaments, ages, and viewpoints that is evident in the novel come across in the journal entries? How is your entry like/different from the partner with whom you worked in the Prewriting exercise?

Name_____

**Directions:** Similarities among characters are sometimes a clue to themes in the story.

1. Place each of the following characters in one or more of the groups below:

| | | | | |
|---|---|---|---|---|
| Jane | Phoebe | Sally | Stradlater | James Castle |
| D.B. | Allie | Mr. Antolini | Dick Slagle | Mr. Spencer |
| Ackley | nuns | singing boy | boys in museum | Lillian Simmons |
| Sunny | Carl Luce | Holden | | |

| Phonies | Innocents | Betrayers |
|---------|-----------|-----------|
|         |           |           |

| Seducers | Outcasts | Materialists |
|----------|----------|--------------|
|          |          |              |

2. Pick one grouping and write an essay on the following:
   What do you think Salinger is saying about people in this group? What common experiences or attitudes are shared by all members of the particular group you chose? Do these characters cope with their problems in similar ways? Do they have similar values? What generalizations might Salinger be making?

Name_____

**Directions:** A symbol is something that stands for something else. For example, the dove is a symbol of peace. Titles, repeated phrases or repeated references to particular objects in a story are often clues to symbols. Symbols are used to emphasize the theme or message of a story.

Throughout *The Catcher in the Rye* there are repeated references to the red cap, to the Robert Burns poem, to the ducks, to the museum, and to "phonies." You can tell that the catcher's mitt and the carrousel also have special significance for Holden; he chooses to write about the former, and he ends his story with the latter.

1.  List as many references to each of these as you can find.

| Reference | Page Numbers |
|---|---|
| red cap | |
| title poem | |
| ducks | |
| museum | |
| phonies | |
| baseball mitt | |
| carrousel | |

2.  How are the red cap and the baseball mitt alike? How are they different?

3.  Choose two of the "phonies." How are they alike? How are they different?

4.  How is Allie like the boy singing "The Catcher in the Rye"? How are they different?

5.  How are the museum mummies like the carrousel animals and the ducks? How are they different?

**Choose one of the pairs in 2-5 and make a Venn diagram for comparison.**

Name_____

**Directions:** Venn diagrams are a helpful way to compare and contrast characters, symbols, settings, themes, and other elements of literature. On lines **A** and **B**, write the two elements you are comparing. In the circle for **A**, write the details that are true only for **A**. In the circle for **B**, write the things that are true only for **B**. In the overlapping area, write details that are true for **both** A and B.

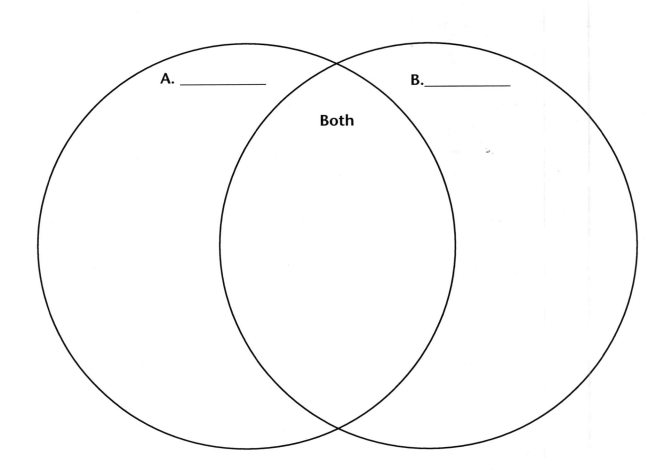

A. _____     B._____

**Both**

Name_____

**Directions:** Trace any one of the following themes throughout *The Catcher in the Rye*. Explain what you think Salinger's message is about the theme that you choose.

- change
- alienation
- courage
- maturing
- honesty

Before you begin writing, use the diagram below or a Venn diagram, or both, to make notes about what you will want to include in your essay.

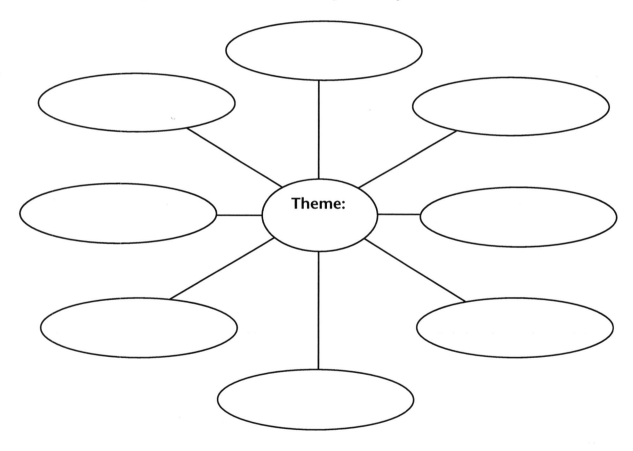

---

Name_____

**Directions:** Many arguments have been made for censoring *The Catcher in the Rye*—and for continuing to teach it.

1. Complete the following chart by filling in reasons for and against censoring this novel.

| For | Against |
|---|---|
| | |

2. In your opinion, should *The Catcher in the Rye* be censored?

3. Write an essay in which you defend or refute the thesis: "*The Catcher in the Rye* should not be censored. It is a novel from which high school students can benefit."

   You might use some of the following phrases, revising as you wish. Use details from the chart above as supportive evidence. Be sure not only to "build your case," but also to provide evidence that contradicts your opponents'.

   *The Catcher in the Rye* should/should not be censored.
   First of all,…          In almost every case,…          Another reason…
   In addition,…          My most important reason…
   Contrary to what the book's detractors/defenders have to say,…

**Directions:** In each circle is a word or phrase that might be used to characterize Holden. In the attached rectangle, summarize an action or comment that demonstrates the characteristic; cite page numbers if possible. (Small groups might assign a few traits to each member, discuss the results within the small group, then share with the whole class.)

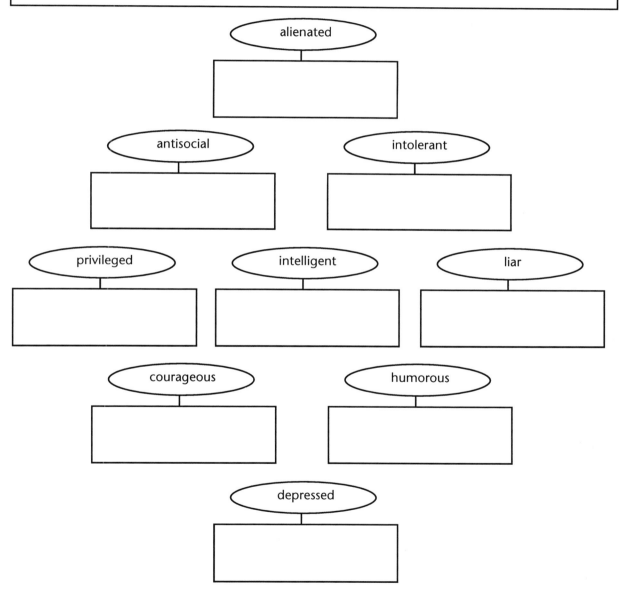

Name_____

**Directions:** Assume the persona of Holden. Write a poem about yourself. See yourself as you were at different times and places. Include some statements, questions, and exclamations. Feel free to complain, shout, laugh, weep, and talk with others in the poem. Capture your personality in the poem. (You might want to experiment with different voices—conveying how different people see you—Mr. Spencer, Phoebe, Ackley, Stradlater, Sally, etc. If so, read Wallace Stevens' "Thirteen Ways of Looking at a Blackbird" as a model.)

*When Allie was alive...*

_____
_____
_____

*at Pencey...*

_____
_____
_____

*during that crazy time last Christmas...*

_____
_____
_____

*with Phoebe...*

_____
_____
_____

*and now...*

_____
_____
_____

## I.  Frame story

A. A story-within-a-story is known as a framework or frame story. Two examples of frame stories are *The Canterbury Tales* and *Moby Dick*. Can you list two others?

B. What are the settings of the frame story Holden tells? That is, what time period is covered and what places are described?

C. What can you infer about the setting in which Holden tells the frame story?

D. Does the story return to the frame situation at the end? How?

E. Speculate about why Salinger chose this structure. That is, why wouldn't the story have been as effective if it had simply begun with the scene at Pencey Prep and ended with the scene at the carrousel?

## II.  Picaresque

A. A picaresque is a tale, usually autobiographical, presenting the life story of a rascal. *Don Quixote* is one example. Can you think of another?

B. Seven qualities distinguish the picaresque novel. Explain how *The Catcher in the Rye* does/does not meet each criterion. (Use separate paper.)

(a) Chronicles part of the life of a rogue in the first-person.

(b) Chief figure is from a low social level and of loose character, according to conventional standards.

(c) Very little plot, but rather a series of slightly connected episodes.

(d) Development of character does not take place; the central figure starts and ends as a rogue; if there is change, it is usually due to circumstance, not character development

(e) Realistic method, plain language, freedom in vocabulary, vividness of detail

(f) Satire is prominent; the main character learns the frailties and foibles of a number of other characters; social and/or national peculiarities may be satirized.

(g) Hero stops short of being a criminal.

**True-False** (8 points each): Write "T" if the statement is true. Write "F" if the statement is false.

_____  1.  The narrator is Holden, a 17-year-old who was kicked out of prep school a few months ago, around Christmas.

_____  2.  Holden goes to see Mr. Spencer because he feels he deserves a higher grade in history.

_____  3.  Holden buys a catcher's mitt while in New York with the fencing team.

_____  4.  Holden thinks that Stradlater is handsome but stuck up.

_____  5.  Holden writes a composition for Stradlater about the red hunting cap.

_____  6.  Holden feels nervous when he thinks about Jane being on a date with Stradlater.

_____  7.  Allie is Holden's younger brother who died of leukemia four years earlier.

_____  8.  Holden lies to the woman on the train about her son's popularity at Pencey.

_____  9.  Holden dances with three women in the nightclub of his hotel.

_____  10.  Holden wonders what happens to the fish in the lagoon when the water freezes.

**Short Answer** (10 points each)

11. Describe two times Holden gets beaten up and explain why these are or are not evidence that he is a coward.


12. List or briefly describe five people Holden considers phonies.


_____     _____


_____     _____


_____

Name_____

**Directions:** Answer each question below in a sentence or two. (4 points each)

1. Briefly describe the narrator of the novel.

2. Name two books or authors the narrator enjoys.

3. What is Pencey and why is Holden leaving?

4. Why does Holden regret going to see Mr. Spencer?

5. Briefly describe Holden's hat and where he got it.

6. How does Holden treat Ackley?

7. Who is Allie?

8. Why does Holden tear up the composition he wrote for Stradlater?

9. What sort of lies does Holden tell on the train and why?

10. Where does Holden direct the taxi to go and why?

11. How does Holden feel about the three women with whom he dances?

12. Who is Phoebe?

13. What is Phoebe like?

14. Why does Holden call his brother D. B. a "prostitute"?

15. What does Holden wonder about the ducks?

16. Why doesn't Holden have any gloves?

17. How is Holden's treatment of the prostitute like his treatment of the burlesque dancer he telephones?

18. Do you think that Holden drinks too much? Briefly explain.

19. Why does Maurice beat up Holden?

20. Why doesn't Holden report Maurice to the police?

**Identification:** Find a character on the right who matches the description on the left. Write the letter of the character next to the matching number. Each character is to be used only once.

_____ 1. Holden took this date to the show with the Lunts.

_____ 2. Pimply and with bad breath, he invited himself into Holden's room frequently.

_____ 3. Holden's younger brother who died of leukemia

_____ 4. the Columbia student who advises Holden to see a psychoanalyst

_____ 5. the friend with whom Holden doesn't trust Stradlater

_____ 6. Holden's older brother, a writer

_____ 7. the boy who jumped out a window rather than take back what he said about someone

_____ 8. the teacher who horrifies Holden by patting him on the head one night

_____ 9. Holden's younger sister

_____ 10. the roommate who called Holden's suitcases "bourgeois"

_____ 11. He has flunked out of several prep schools.

_____ 12. Holden's self-important roommate

_____ 13. Holden's history teacher, who flunked him but wished him luck

A. Holden
B. D. B.
C. Phoebe
D. Allie
E. Sally
F. Jane
G. Ackley
H. Stradlater
I. Mr. Spencer
J. James Castle
K. Carl Luce
L. Mr. Antolini
M. Dick Slagle

**Multiple Choice**
**Directions:** Indicate the BEST response for each item.

1. Holden is telling the story from
   (a) a hotel in New York City       (b) a prep school in Pennsylvania
   (c) a psychiatric center in California (d) a state mental hospital in New England

2. Holden tells what happened around Christmas
   (a) a few days ago              (b) a few months ago
   (c) a few years ago             (d) ten years ago

3. Holden bought the red hat because
   (a) he likes to hunt
   (c) he likes the way he looks in it
   (b) he wanted to give it to his sister
   (d) he needed to replace one that was stolen

4. Holden's opinion of reading is that
   (a) he believes readers are phonies
   (c) he prefers classics like
       *The Return of the Native*
   (b) he likes war stories best
   (d) he reads only magazine stories

5. Holden has been a friend to him, but he turns a deaf ear when Holden needs a friend and a place to sleep.
   (a) Mr. Antolini        (b) Ackley        (c) Stradlater        (d) James Castle

6. Which of these words does NOT describe Stradlater?
   (a) handsome        (b) sensitive        (c) messy        (d) narcissistic

7. Holden takes out the catcher's mitt because he plans to
   (a) show it to Ackley
   (c) memorize the poems on it
   (b) use it to play baseball with Mal Brossard
   (d) write a composition about it

8. Holden thinks that he is a good
   (a) singer        (b) athlete        (c) writer        (d) piano player

9. When Holden learns that Stradlater is dating Jane, Holden feels mainly
   (a) angry with Jane
   (c) bored by the news
   (b) mistrustful of Stradlater
   (d) relieved that Jane has found someone

10. Like Phoebe, Allie
    (a) was always in trouble at school
    (c) often got mad
    (b) seldom laughed
    (d) had red hair

11. When Holden realizes that the woman on the train is the mother of a classmate, he
    (a) stops talking to her
    (b) lies to her about how well her son is doing
    (c) lies to her about all the trouble her son has been in
    (d) tells her honestly how little he liked her son

12. Holden stays at the hotel because he
   (a) enjoys watching the perverts
   (b) knows his parents wouldn't allow him to come home
   (c) is planning to meet Sally there
   (d) doesn't want to face his parents yet

13. When Holden calls the burlesque stripper,
   (a) she tells him to get lost
   (b) she kindly tells him he is too young
   (c) he says he can't meet her any other night
   (d) he arranges to meet her that night

14. Holden kissed Jane
   (a) once when she cried
   (b) once after her date with Stradlater
   (c) often when they played checkers
   (d) often when they drove around in cabs

15. Holden asks the cab drivers where the ducks go
   (a) during hunting season       (b) when the lagoon freezes
   (c) when summer storms blow     (d) when parking lots are built

16. Holden goes to school in Pennsylvania, but his parents live in
   (a) California    (b) Massachusetts    (c) New York       (d) Maine

17. Holden brags about his "terrific capacity" for
   (a) fighting     (b) drinking     (c) attracting women     (d) athleticism

18. Holden is worried that _____ will try to find out if he is Catholic.
   (a) Mr. Antolini          (b) Sally
   (c) the prostitute        (d) the nuns

19. Holden gives _____ $10.
   (a) Mr. Antolini          (b) Sally
   (c) the prostitute        (d) the nuns

20. Holden gets this gift for Phoebe but breaks it.
   (a) a record              (b) a mirror
   (c) a vase                (d) a glass carrousel

21. Sally and Holden fight after Sally refuses to
    (a) kiss him                     (b) go away with him
    (c) go to the show               (d) go skating

22. Holden and Phoebe fight after Holden refuses to
    (a) let Phoebe go away with him   (b) take her to the zoo
    (c) promise to return to school   (d) give back her Christmas money

23. When Phoebe asks what Holden would like to be, he says
    (a) a lawyer                     (b) a writer
    (c) he wants to save children    (d) a dream-chaser

24. Holden fantasizes about pretending to be
    (a) a deaf mute                  (b) a famous actor
    (c) a murderer                   (d) a ghost

25. Holden feels happy at the end as he watches Phoebe
    (a) unpack her suitcase          (b) return to school
    (c) visit the mummies            (d) ride the carrousel

## I. Analysis

**Directions:** Select A or B and write a paragraph with complete sentences and at least three clearly explained examples. Indicate the letter of the question you answer.

**A.** Explain why Holden wants to be a "catcher in the rye."

**B.** Explain how Holden defines "phoniness."

## II. Critical/Creative Thinking

**Directions:** Select C, D, or E. Indicate the letter of the question you are answering.

**C.** You are Phoebe. Write an entry in your journal, the night after you wake up to find that Holden is back and that he has been kicked out of Pencey.

**D.** Write the scene that shows the conversation between the Antolinis the morning after Holden leaves in the middle of the night.

**E.** You are Holden, applying to another prep school. Write an essay on "what I hope to get from my high school education." (Be sure to write from Holden's point of view.)

34

Name_____

*The Catcher in the Rye*
Unit Exam • Level II
Use After Reading

**Identification:** Find a character on the right who matches the description on the left. Write the letter of the character next to the matching number. Each character is to be used only once.

_____ 1. Holden's roommate, he dated Jane.

_____ 2. He gave sex talks while a student adviser at Whooton.

_____ 3. elderly history teacher down with the grippe

_____ 4. pretty girl Holden asked to marry him

_____ 5. He jumped out a window wearing Holden's sweater.

_____ 6. a screenwriter

_____ 7. Holden played checkers with her.

_____ 8. ten-year-old girl who gave Holden her Christmas savings

_____ 9. "about the best teacher" Holden ever had

_____ 10. an intrusive social isolate with halitosis

_____ 11. 17-year-old son of a lawyer

_____ 12. nice, smart red-head who wrote poems on his baseball mitt

_____ 13. Holden was painfully aware that his suitcases were better than this roommate's.

A. Holden
B. D. B.
C. Phoebe
D. Allie
E. Sally
F. Jane
G. Ackley
H. Stradlater
I. Mr. Spencer
J. James Castle
K. Carl Luce
L. Mr. Antolini
M. Dick Slagle

**Multiple Choice**
**Directions:** Indicate the BEST response for each item.

1. Which of the following words does NOT describe Holden Caulfield?
   (a) humorless    (b) defiant    (c) depressed    (d) alienated

2. Which of the following jobs would Holden be LEAST likely to choose when he is 21?
   (a) counseling depressed teens    (b) writing screenplays
   (c) park ranger    (d) teaching second grade

3. Which of the following best describes Holden's treatment of Ackley?
   (a) contemptuous            (b) pitying
   (c) tolerant                (d) admiring

4. Holden's reaction when he learns that Stradlater is dating Jane is most similar to the reaction of a(n)
   (a) encouraging father          (b) friend experiencing vicarious pleasure
   (c) jealous rival of Stradlater's   (d) protective big brother of Jane's

5. If Holden found himself at a debutante ball he would probably
   (a) wear his red hunter's cap      (b) make loud jokes about the women
   (c) go through the appropriate     (d) defy convention by refusing to dance
       "motions"

6. Holden tears up the composition because he
   (a) is pained by the memories of Allie      (b) knows that he has written a
       it evokes                                   "phony" paper
   (c) realizes that Stradlater does not        (d) decides that it is wrong to do
       appreciate it                                Stradlater's assignment

7. Regarding Allie, Holden gives the impression that he
   (a) feels a lingering sense of loss      (b) is angry at Allie for "leaving"
   (c) is pretending that Allie never       (d) feels a guilty sense of relief that
       existed                                  Allie is gone

8. Like Allie, James Castle
   (a) was well-liked by everyone          (b) frequently borrowed Holden's
                                               clothes
   (c) pretended to be happier than he was   (d) died young

9. Holden's comment to Phoebe that he would like to be a "catcher in the rye" demonstrates he is
   (a) quixotic    (b) mendacious    (c) materialistic    (d) self-interested

10. Holden gives money to the nuns because he
    (a) can't bring himself to refuse their request
    (b) has decided to try to live without money
    (c) hears a voice telling him to give to God
    (d) feels that they need the money

11. After dancing with the three women, Holden feels mainly
   (a) uplifted by their naivete
   (b) angered by their condescension
   (c) depressed by the emptiness of their lives
   (d) outraged by their willingness to let him pay

12. Holden's childhood memories show that the thing he enjoys most about the museum is that it
   (a) has rotating exhibits
   (b) admits children for free
   (c) teaches children things they don't learn in school
   (d) seldom changes

13. Holden's conversations with the taxi drivers about the ducks shows that Holden
   (a) has compassion for helpless, innocent creatures
   (b) enjoys baiting taxi drivers
   (c) observes animals more closely than people
   (d) can't stop telling lies once he starts

14. Holden goes out with Sally because he
   (a) thinks she is something she is not
   (b) believes that she is not a phony
   (c) loves her and feels that he can change her
   (d) seeks company and is willing to tolerate phoniness

15. The structure of *The Catcher in the Rye* is best described as
   (a) a narrative with several flashbacks
   (b) a stream of consciousness novel with little chronological order
   (c) a satire composed of disconnected vignettes
   (d) a story-within-a-story with a few flashbacks

16. Holden Caulfield is most like
   (a) Peter Pan
   (b) Captain Hook
   (c) Wendy's father
   (d) one of Wendy's brothers

17. Holden tells Phoebe about his catcher-in-the-rye fantasy: "I'm standing on the edge of some crazy _____."
   (a) field     (b) quicksand     (c) roof     (d) cliff

18. When Holden leaves Mr. Antolini's, Holden feels mainly
   (a) angry     (b) upset     (c) curious     (d) joyful

---

19. Holden does NOT describe himself as a(n)
    (a) pacifist    (b) liar    (c) adult    (d) coward

20. Which of the following best describes how the narrator treats his audience?
    (a) gives the reader a friendly invitation to come close
    (b) muses inwardly as if unaware that he has an audience
    (c) acts resentful of the audience's intrusion
    (d) keeps the audience at a distance by taking an objective stance

21. The reader can best infer that socioeconomically, Holden's family
    (a) was once poor and uneducated
    (b) is in the middle class
    (c) is privileged and wealthy
    (d) is nouveau-riche

22. Regarding Holden's plan to hitch out west and take a job at a filling station, the reader can best infer at the end that
    (a) Holden is on his way out west right now
    (b) Holden plans to go west in a couple of months
    (c) Holden's parents intervened in the plan
    (d) Holden followed through but tired of the work

23. Holden tells Allie to go get his bike because Holden
    (a) feels guilty about not taking Allie along years ago
    (b) sometimes forgets momentarily that Allie is dead
    (c) is having suicidal thoughts about joining Allie
    (d) mistakenly refers to Phoebe by her dead brother's name

24. Which of the following best characterizes Holden's swearing?
    (a) motivated by the urge to seem "one of the boys"
    (b) indicative of desperate bravado
    (c) designed to offend
    (d) mild and occasional

25. Holden's tone at the end of the story, as he reflects on having told so many people about "this madman stuff" is
    (a) bitter and hostile
    (b) regretful and lonely
    (c) relieved and light-hearted
    (d) determined and optimistic

## I. Analysis

**Directions:** Select A or B and indicate the letter of the question you decide to answer. Choose the alternative that best represents your opinion. Explain the reasons for your choice in a short paragraph on a separate sheet of paper. Cite evidence from the book to support your opinion.

A. By lying to the mother on the train, Holden reveals his
   (1) problem as a pathological liar
   (2) compassion
   (3) other

B. Which of the following books would Holden say he enjoyed most?
   (1) *A Separate Peace* (Knowles)
   (2) *A Solitary Blue* (Voigt)
   (3) some other book you have read, not mentioned in the novel

## II. Critical and Creative Thinking

**Directions:** Select C, D, or E.

C. Write a flashback in which Holden recalls meeting you. Be sure to connect the flashback with some present action mentioned in the story. (Tell what evokes the memory.) Also, make it clear whether Holden likes you or considers you a "phony."

D. Write an essay on the possible symbolic meaning of the ducks in *The Catcher in the Rye,* or choose another symbol from the novel for your essay.

E. You are Holden, applying to another Prep school. Write an essay to accompany your application that tells about the person or event that has had the most significant impact on your life.

# Answer Key

**Note:** Many of the activities are designed to elicit open-ended responses and therefore have no answer key entry.

**Activity #1:** Encourage students to share and discuss their answers.

**Activity #2:** <u>Sample:</u>

**Visual:**

**Synonyms**
excluded
isolated
segregated

**OSTRACIZED**

kept out of
the inner
circle

The other tribe members
ostracized the rule-breaker
by making him live outside
of their camp.

**Activity #3:** 1-halitosis; 2-pacifist; 3-exhibitionist; 4-half nelson

**Activity #4:** 1-immaterial (irrelevant); the other three mean required; 2-jitterbugging (dancing); the other three have to do with including and excluding; 3-aimless (without a goal); the other three are positive descriptions of being; 4. conversationalist (skilled at engaging in dialogue); the other three refer to dressers; 5. muscular (strong); the other three have to do with name-recognition; 6. ostentation (showiness); the other three have to do with proof

**Activity #5:** (There will be some variation in answers, but responses should reflect student's understanding that a rake is a scoundrel, but not usually cruel; a chateau is a castle in France or in a French-speaking country; a clavichord is a small, early keyboard instrument.)

**Activity #6:** 1-clique; 2-spendthrift; 3-bourgeois; 4-raspy; 5-prejudiced; 6-mutinying; 7-spendthrift; 8-raspy; 9-prejudiced; 10-mutinying

**Activity #7:** 1-boisterous; 2-kettle drums; 3-inferiority complex; 4-psychoanalyst; 5-putrid; 6-sacrilegious; 7-inane; 8-atheist; 9-celebrity; 10-aristocratic; 11-spiritual; 12-economizing

**Activity #8:** 1-double decker; 2-harrowing; 3-reciprocal; 4-humility; 5-intellectual; 6-provocative; 7-unsanitary; 8-unify; 9-pedagogical; 10-stenographer

**Activity #9:** Webs will vary, but should mention that Holden is now 17, has some gray hair, is tall for his age, curses a lot, seems alienated, is quite sarcastic and makes critical comments about others, but actually acts quite compassionate and sensitive.

**Activities #10-19** are open-ended.

**Comprehension Quiz Level I**

1-T; 2-F; 3-F; 4-T; 5-F; 6-T; 7-T; 8-T; 9-T; 10-T; 11-He fights Stradlater while "defending Jane's honor" and he fights the pimp while refusing to fork over money he didn't owe. 12-Ackley, Stradlater, the alumnus who spoke to the students; Lillian Simmons; any of the three women in the hotel nightclub.

**Comprehension Quiz Level II**

1. Holden Caulfield, 17-year-old who has just flunked out of prep school and had some sort of nervous breakdown
2. Out of Africa and Return of the Native
3. prep school in Pennsylvania—Holden has failing grades.
4. Mr. Spencer lectures him about his flunking and wishes him "good luck."
5. red hunting hat with a long brim he bought in NEW YORK CITY.
6. honestly and directly, with some offer of friendship
7. Holden's younger brother who died of leukemia
8. Stradlater yells at Holden that the paper doesn't fit the assignment.
9. Holden tells a classmate's mother that the boy is popular.
10. to a seedy hotel because he doesn't want to face his parents yet
11. He feels sorry for them.

12. Holden's younger sister, whom he loves a lot.
13. Spunky, bright, verbal, likes to act and write, loves her brother.
14. He doesn't approve of D. B.'s using his writing talents to write screenplays—he thinks movies and actors are phony.
15. what happens to them when the lagoon freezes
16. Someone stole them.
17. He doesn't follow through on his intentions with either one.
18. Student opinion—should be explained.
19. He wants an extra $5.
20. He doesn't want anyone to know he arranged for a prostitute.

## Unit Exam, Level I

**Identification:** 1-e; 2-g; 3-d; 4-k; 5-f; 6-b; 7-j; 8-l; 9-c; 10-m; 11-a; 12-h; 13-i
**Multiple Choice:** 1-c; 2-b; 3-c; 4-c; 5-b; 6-b; 7-d; 8-c; 9-b; 10-d; 11-b; 12-d; 13-c; 14-a; 15-b; 16-c; 17-b; 18-d; 19-d; 20-a; 21-b; 22-a; 23-c; 24-a; 25-d

### I. Analysis:

**A.** Students who choose A should point out that Holden likes children, wants to protect them, doesn't want to grow up.
**B.** Students who choose B should explain that Holden considers "phony" attempts to impress others with a "public" face that hides one's real feelings—hypocrisy.

### II. Critical Thinking and Creative Writing

**C.** Phoebe's entry should reveal her love of Holden, and her fears about how their father will react.
**D.** The conversation should probably include Mr. Antolini's explanation as to why Holden left so precipitously
**E.** The essay should address the question, but also reflect Holden's tendency to "digress" and his confusion about what he wants from school.

## Unit Exam, Level II

**Identification:** 1-h; 2-k; 3-i; 4-e; 5-j; 6-b; 7-f; 8-c; 9-l; 10-g; 11-a; 12-d; 13-m
**Multiple Choice:** 1-a; 2-b; 3-c; 4-d; 5-c; 6-c; 7-a; 8-d; 9-a; 10-d; 11-c; 12-d; 13-a; 14-d; 15-d; 16-a; 17-d; 18-b; 19-c; 20-a; 21-c; 22-c; 23-a; 24-b; 25-b

### I. Analysis

**A.** Students who choose (a) may point out that Holden talks about his inability to stop lying once he starts; he also keeps the truth from others—like his parents. Students who choose (b) may point out that it gives Holden pleasure to make the mother feel good about her son.
**B.** (a) Holden might well identify with the compassionate, alienated prep school student, now grown, who narrates *A Separate Peace*. (d) Likewise, Holden might like reading about an honest young man struggling to grow up and to deal with his parents' divorce (*A Solitary Blue*).

### II. Critical and Creative Thinking

**C.** The flashback should connect with present action (for example, Holden's view of someone's shoes might remind him of your shoes) and should reveal Holden's opinion of the student—in language that Holden might use.
**D.** The essay should clearly present a thesis (that addresses Holden's resistance to change, his unwillingness to grow up, and his fascination with death as a way to "freeze" childhood innocence and integrity) and should support that thesis with plenty of detail from the story.
**E.** The essay should answer the question, but should also reflect Holden's tendency to "digress." Allie might well be mentioned.

## Study Guide

(Students' answers may not match exactly. Some questions are open-ended.)

**Chapter 1**
1. Holden Caulfield; "the madman stuff that happened to me around Christmas"
2. Holden's older brother, now writing screenplays, which Holden considers a dishonorable profession.
3. Holden's school, a fashionable prep school

---

4. He is flunking four subjects; he doesn't seem to care too much.
## Chapter 2
1. Holden's history teacher; to say good-bye, since Mr. Spencer is sick
2. six foot two, gray hairs
3. Spencer is probably trying to wake up Holden; Holden is embarrassed and thinks it's a dirty trick.
4. other schools Holden has flunked out of; He claims they were full of phonies.
## Chapter 3
1. a red hunting hat
2. Thomas Hardy, Somerset Maugham, Ring Lardner, Isak Dinesen
3. a pimply outcast from next door; not really, but Holden tolerates him
4. Holden's roommate—the well-dressed, handsome jock type.
## Chapter 4
1. to write a composition for him
2. Jane Gallagher
3. He "practically lived next door to her the summer before last." They played checkers, talked a lot. Holden is jealous and protective.
## Chapter 5
1. to Agerstown with Mal and Ackley; They eat, play pinballs, go back to the dorm.
2. Allie's mitt, which has poems written all over it to keep him from being bored in the outfield.
3. Holden's little brother, who died of leukemia, was smart, well-liked, and easy-going. Holden was crazy about him.
4. 1946 /4 years/ 17 at the time of writing, 16 at the time of the book's story-within-a-story / If Allie had lived, he would be 14 or 15 now.
## Chapter 6
1. He fears Stradlater took advantage of Jane.
2. He thinks it doesn't fulfill the assignment. Holden tears it up; they fight; Stradlater wins.
## Chapter 7
1. He doesn't want to be in the room with Stradlater.
2. He's being sarcastic—he really thinks Ackley is rude, stupid, and not much of a friend.
3. There seems to be little reason to stay—and no place he can comfortably sleep. He plans to go to a hotel in NYC for a few days.
## Chapter 8
1. the mother of a schoolmate Holden detests, Ernest Morrow
2. that he's sensitive, popular, and humble; to make his mother feel good
3. He says he has to have an operation.
## Chapter 9
1. D. B., Phoebe, Jane's mother, Sally Hayes, Carl Luce
2. where they go when the lagoon freezes
3. a cross-dresser; a couple with a "water fetish"
4. Holden says he won't "horse around" with a girl he doesn't like; he doesn't know why, but he always breaks his rules.
5. a former burlesque stripper; He was hoping to get her to meet him by saying this was his only available night, but she was unwilling.
## Chapter 10
1. She's pretty, smart, affectionate, and writes books.
2. He ordered a scotch and soda, but with no I. D. he had to settle for Coke.
3. He finds them homely, pathetic, and depressing.
## Chapter 11
1. Answers vary.
2. She wasn't a phony.
## Chapter 12
1. the obnoxious taxi driver; the ducks and fish in the winter

2. a Black jazz pianist and owner of a "joint" in the village; Holden finds him phony because of his fake "humility" still, Holden would like to be seen as one of Ernie's friends.

3. a friend of D. B.'s; She's a phony.

4. In order to get away from Lillian, Holden has to leave Ernie's.

**Chapter 13**

1. Not much—possibly he'd search the suspected thief's room and take back the gloves. He'd rather not fight.

2. depressed

3. He agrees to pay a prostitute $5 for "a throw;" He changes his mind once he sees her.

**Chapter 14**

1. He "talks" to Allie when he's depressed; speaking as if Allie is alive is comforting, plus Holden needs to relieve some of his guilt over not always taking Allie with him.

2. He's "sort of an atheist."

3. Maurice, the elevator-operator/pimp, claims Holden owes another $5.

4. Holden felt like jumping out the window, committing suicide.

**Chapter 15**

1. Sally is a girl Holden has dated before who comes from a good family and knows a lot about literature and art. Holden "used to think she was intelligent."

2. Answers vary. (He is a lawyer, quite wealthy.)

3. The nuns Holden spoke with at the train station had inexpensive luggage just like Dick Slagle.

4. Holden likes the nuns because they seem genuine and unaffected. They are kind to him and think he's a nice boy.

**Chapter 16**

1. He wants to find a recording of "Little Shirley Beans" for his sister, Phoebe.

2. "If a body catch a body coming through the rye." Holden likes the little boy and feels happier.

3. He finds live shows less appalling than movies, but thinks all actors are phony and egotistical.

4. Holden liked the way nothing at the museum changed—you could look forward to seeing something and it would be there. He doesn't like change much.

**Chapter 17**

1. A boy Holden roomed with at Elkton Hills, Harris was a bore. the Lunts, Sally

2. At that moment, he feels like he does. She answers that she loves him too but doesn't really mean it.

3. He called the Lunts "angels."

4. Sally wants to; they have a fight and Holden leaves her there.

**Chapter 18**

1. He doesn't find it religious or pretty, but thinks Jesus might have liked the drummer.

2. Holden found the movie "putrid."

3. Army life doesn't appeal to him at all, but he wouldn't mind dying.

**Chapter 19**

1. from the Whooton School/ intellectual ones

2. He sometimes acted "very flitty"—but Holden probably hopes for some advice.

3. a psychoanalyst

**Chapter 20**

1. He pretends he's been shot in the stomach.

2. He is extremely drunk. She tells him to go home and go to sleep.

3. Phoebe's record breaks.

4. He was in the hospital because when Allie died he had smashed all the windows in the garage with his bare fists.

**Chapter 21**

1. He reads her notebook.

2. She hugs and kisses him; she tells him about her part in the play, about a movie she saw, that their father has to fly to California, and that D. B. may be coming for Christmas.

3. It was her reaction to realizing that Holden had been kicked out of Pencey.

## Chapter 22
1. He says Pencey is full of mean guys and phonies.
2. a boy at Elkton Hills who jumped out the window rather than take back something he had said (and meant) about another boy
3. Allie and talking with Phoebe, who says Allie doesn't count because he's dead.
4. Holden thinks lawyers are hot shots who play golf and bridge and drink martinis, and this doesn't appeal to him. This is how he sees his father.
5. "a catcher in the rye" who saves children from falling off a cliff that is next to a field of rye where they are playing; He would have liked to have saved Allie, and he may be thinking that he himself is heading for a fall and wishes someone would catch him.

## Chapter 23
1. A former English teacher, Holden likes him because he's young and you can kid around with him.
2. They dance to the music on the radio.
3. her Christmas money
4. to Mr. Antolini's; They won't find out about his expulsion until then.

## Chapter 24
1. Antolini tells Holden he's afraid he's given up before he ever started looking. Antolini is more philosophical and analytical than Spencer, but the message is similar.
2. a psychoanalyst who said, "The mark of the immature man is that he wants to die nobly for a cause, while the mark of the mature man is that he wants to live humbly for one."
3. Antolini is patting his head.

## Chapter 25
1. Grand Central Station
2. He thinks he looks like he shouldn't, according to the article.
3. The guys are swearing about the Christmas tree, totally counter to the feelings that are supposed to prevail at Christmas.
4. He felt too sick.
5. He begins to feel disoriented.
6. He decides he'll go out West, perhaps even pretend to be a deaf mute.
7. He wants to leave a note for Phoebe to meet him. He hates to see innocence corrupted.
8. He likes them, as he does Phoebe, the skater, and the little boy who was singing.
9. She wants to run away with him.
10. Partly to make up with Phoebe, but also to start facing reality.
11. the zoo
12. The simplicity of Phoebe's happiness makes him happy. He identifies, misses his youth.

## Chapter 26
1. He "got sick" and was sent out to California for psychological help. Perhaps these are memories too painful to relive.
2. in the fall
3. in a psychiatric institution of some kind
4. his English girlfriend; He asks him how he feels about all that's happened.
5. Answers will vary.